The TÂO and its Characteristics

Lao-Tse

Translated by James Legge

With a new foreword by Graham Earnshaw

The Tâo And Its Characteristics

By Lao-Tse, translated by James Legge

ISBN-13: 978-988-8273-86-7

HISTORY / Asia / China

EB104

Published by Earnshaw Books Ltd. (Hong Kong)

INTRODUCTION

THE TAOIST CLASSIC romanized variously as the Dedejing, Taoteching, the Tao Teh King and quite a few other alternatives (道德經), is one of the great philosophical treatises of all time and has been translated into English many times. Whether Taoism is actually a religion or not, and whether Laozi, the supposed author of the tract, actually existed, are beside the point. this text, dating from well over two thousand years ago, has much to say that has value for all humanity in all ages.

China has much to offer the world, but the most valuable, in my opinion, are the twin schools of thoughts embodied in Taoism and Confucianism. Confucianism, simply put, concerns relationships between human beings and the structure of societies and other groupings of people. Taoism, equally simply put, is about how humanity relates in the universe. Neither are strictly religions and both developed in isolation from the religious and philosophical trends in the rest of the Euroasian landmass. Earnshaw Books is starting a new series of books which will reprint the most important of the Chinese classics, all with the original Chinese text included for reference. We are mostly choosing classic translations not just to save money, but also because these translations were done in the first flush of the intellectual connection between the modern West and the ancient East, and at a time when the understanding of the old texts by the Chinese scholars assisting in the work was at its height.

It is appropriate to begin the series with the Daodejing

because of its fundamental impact on Chinese thought and behavior for over two millennia. While Confucianism created the structure of Chinese society, the elephant in the room has always been Taoism, and trying to understand Taoism is the single most valuable thing anyone looking to unlock the mysery of Chineseness can do. It is the idea of there being a Way, a harmonic center to the Universe with all things benefitting in cleaving to that way and suffering by leaving it; the idea of inaction and action having equal impact ... There is much here to ponder.

James Legge was a Scotsman, born in 1815, who played an enormously important role in introducing, integrating and explaining China's classics and the wisdom they include into the global mainstream of thought. He translated, with the help of Chinese assistants, virtually all of the great works from China's past including the Confucian analects (論語), the works of Mencius and the Book of Songs (詩經). He also did the two most puzzling, but possibly the most significant all the Chinese classics, the Book of Changes (易經) and the Taoist manual, the Daodejing.

Legge came to Asia at the age of twenty-four as a missionary, and first spent three years in Malacca before moving to Hong Kong where he lived for thirty years. While in Malacca, he began his life's work, convinced that if Christianity was to be successful in China, the missionaries had to have a full and accurate understanding of Chinese philosophy and thinking. To his great credit, and no doubt his own satisfaction, he completed this huge work before his death in 1897.

In 1876, he became the first Professor of Chinese at Oxford University, a post he held until his death. During those years, he also collaborated with the German-born scholar Max Müller in the preparation of the ground-breaking "Sacred Books of the East" series, a total of fifty books covering a wide range range of translations of works from India, China and beyond. It was in this collection that Legge's translation of the Daodejing was first published.

His was not the first translation, nor was it the last. The first known version in English was done by another Scottish missionary named John Chalmers, published in 1868. Legge's effort at explaining this Work was published in 1891. Probably the best-known and most-consulted of the more classical translations is that done by Lin Yu-tang in his book The Wisdom of Lao-tzu published in 1948. Legge had neither the benefit of the innate Chinese instincts of Lin, or the benefit of research in later decades, including the materials found in the Mawangdui tomb site near Changsha in Hunan Province in the early 1970s. But Legge's translation is still in many ways the baseline of Western understanding of this and many other Chinese works.

Interest in Taoism has always been overshadowed by the Confucian classics, and also Buddhism, but it has played a fundamental role in the development of Chinese culture. Confucianism stresses the importance of structure in life and society while Taoism represents the importance of non-structure – creativity, emptiness and randomness. Taoism, it can be argued, is a body of thought, a way of conceiving of the world, that is on a deeper, more complex level of sophistication than any other system yet devised by human beings anywhere at any time.

Legge breaks the "chapters" or sections of the work into a series of numbered "verses", probably with the idea of mimicking the organization of the King James Bible. But it is important to remember that no such divisions into verses existed in the original Chinese. Traditional Chinese included no punctuation at all, which is one of the primary causes of confusion and differences of interpretation.

His approach to the translation is a mixture of meaning

transfer through to English prose and occasional flourishes of poetry. There is a sense that he would have much preferred to do the whole thing as poetry if he could only have made it fit. As it is, the rhyming lines act as choruses interspersing the rest of the verse-like content.

Some of the English in this translation today has a feel of quaintness, but at the time, it set a new watermark in terms of the depth of understanding of the concepts hidden within the obscure phraseology from more than two thousands years ago, and is still essential reading for people today trying to figure out the Way.

Graham Earnshaw
China
October 2017

PART I

CHAPTER 1

觀妙章

1. 1. The Tâo that can be trodden is not the enduring and unchanging Tâo. The name that can be named is not the enduring and unchanging name.

道可道，非常道。名可名，非常名。

1. 2. (Conceived of as) having no name, it is the Originator of heaven and earth; (conceived of as) having a name, it is the Mother of all things.

無，名天地之始；有，名萬物之母。

1. 3. Always without desire we must be found,
If its deep mystery we would sound;
But if desire always within us be,
Its outer fringe is all that we shall see.

故常無，欲以觀其妙；常有，欲以觀其徼。

1. 4. Under these two aspects, it is really the same; but as development takes place, it receives the different names. Together we call them the Mystery. Where the Mystery is the deepest is the gate of all that is subtle and wonderful.

此兩者，同出而異名，同謂之玄。玄之又玄，眾妙之門。

CHAPTER 2
觀徼章

2.1. All in the world know the beauty of the beautiful, and in doing this they have (the idea of) what ugliness is; they all know the skill of the skilful, and in doing this they have (the idea of) what the want of skill is.

天下皆知美之爲美，斯惡已。皆知善之爲善，斯不善已。

2.2. So it is that existence and non-existence give birth the one to (the idea of) the other; that difficulty and ease produce the one (the idea of) the other; that length and shortness fashion out the one the figure of the other; that (the ideas of) height and lowness arise from the contrast of the one with the other; that the musical notes and tones become harmonious through the relation of one with another; and that being before and behind give the idea of one following another.

故有無相生，難易相成，長短相形，高下相傾，音聲相和，前后相隨。

2.3. Therefore the sage manages affairs without doing anything, and conveys his instructions without the use of speech.

是以聖人處無爲之事，行不言之敎；

2. 4. All things spring up, and there is not one which declines to show itself; they grow, and there is no claim made for their ownership; they go through their processes, and there is no expectation (of a reward for the results). The work is accomplished, and there is no resting in it (as an achievement).
萬物作焉而不辭，生而不有，爲而不恃，功成而不居。

2. 5. The work is done, but how no one can see;
'Tis this that makes the power not cease to be.
夫唯弗居，是以不去。

CHAPTER 3
安民章

3.1. Not to value and employ men of superior ability is the way to keep the people from rivalry among themselves; not to prize articles which are difficult to procure is the way to keep them from becoming thieves; not to show them what is likely to excite their desires is the way to keep their minds from disorder.

不尚賢，使民不爭；不貴難得之貨，使民不為盜；不見可欲，使民心不亂。

3.2. Therefore the sage, in the exercise of his government, empties their minds, fills their bellies, weakens their wills, and strengthens their bones.

是以聖人之治，虛其心，實其腹，弱其志，強其骨。

3.3. He constantly (tries to) keep them without knowledge and without desire, and where there are those who have knowledge, to keep them from presuming to act (on it). When there is this abstinence from action, good order is universal.

常使民無知無欲。使夫智者不敢為也。為無為，則無不治。

CHAPTER 4
不盈章

4.1. The Tâo is (like) the emptiness of a vessel; and in our employment of it we must be on our guard against all fulness. How deep and unfathomable it is, as if it were the Honoured Ancestor of all things!

道沖，而用之或不盈。淵兮似萬物之宗；

4.2. We should blunt our sharp points, and unravel the complications of things; we should attemper our brightness, and bring ourselves into agreement with the obscurity of others. How pure and still the Tâo is, as if it would ever so continue!

挫其銳，解其紛，和其光，同其塵，湛兮似或存。

4.3. I do not know whose son it is. It might appear to have been before God.

吾不知誰之子，象帝之先。

CHAPTER 5
守中章

5. 1. Heaven and earth do not act from (the impulse of) any wish to be benevolent; they deal with all things as the dogs of grass are dealt with. The sages do not act from (any wish to be) benevolent; they deal with the people as the dogs of grass are dealt with.

天地不仁，以萬物為芻狗；聖人不仁，以百姓為芻狗。

5. 2. May not the space between heaven and earth be compared to a bellows?

天地之間，其猶橐籥乎？

5. 3 'Tis emptied, yet it loses not its power;
'Tis moved again, and sends forth air the more.
Much speech to swift exhaustion lead we see;
Your inner being guard, and keep it free.

虛而不屈，動而愈出。多言數窮，不如守中。

CHAPTER 6

谷神章

6.1. The valley spirit dies not, aye the same;
The female mystery thus do we name.
Its gate, from which at first they issued forth,
Is called the root from which grew heaven and earth.
Long and unbroken does its power remain,
Used gently, and without the touch of pain.

谷神不死，是謂玄牝。玄牝之門，是謂天地根。綿綿若存，用之不勤。

CHAPTER 7
無私章

7. 1. Heaven is long-enduring and earth continues long. The reason why heaven and earth are able to endure and continue thus long is because they do not live of, or for, themselves. This is how they are able to continue and endure.

天長地久。 天地所以骽長且久者，以其不自
生，故骽長生。

7. 2. Therefore the sage puts his own person last, and yet it is found in the foremost place; he treats his person as if it were foreign to him, and yet that person is preserved. Is it not because he has no personal and private ends, that therefore such ends are realised?

是以聖人后其身而身先；外其身而身存。 非以
其無私邪？ 故骽成其私。

CHAPTER 8
若水章

8. 1. The highest excellence is like (that of) water. The excellence of water appears in its benefiting all things, and in its occupying, without striving (to the contrary), the low place which all men dislike. Hence (its way) is near to (that of) the Tâo.
上善若水。水善利萬物而不爭，處眾人之所惡，故幾于道。

8. 2. The excellence of a residence is in (the suitability of) the place; that of the mind is in abysmal stillness; that of associations is in their being with the virtuous; that of government is in its securing good order; that of (the conduct of) affairs is in its ability; and that of (the initiation of) any movement is in its timeliness.
居善地，心善淵，與善仁，言善信，政善治，事善能，動善時。

8. 3. And when (one with the highest excellence) does not wrangle (about his low position), no one finds fault with him.
夫唯不爭，故無尤。

CHAPTER 9
持盈章

9. 1. It is better to leave a vessel unfilled, than to attempt to carry it when it is full. If you keep feeling a point that has been sharpened, the point cannot long preserve its sharpness.

持而盈之，不如其已；揣而銳之，不可長保。

9. 2. When gold and jade fill the hall, their possessor cannot keep them safe. When wealth and honours lead to arrogancy, this brings its evil on itself. When the work is done, and one's name is becoming distinguished, to withdraw into obscurity is the way of Heaven.

金玉滿堂，莫之能守；富貴而驕，自遺其咎。
功成身退，天之道。

CHAPTER 10

嬰兒章

10. 1. When the intelligent and animal souls are held together in one embrace, they can be kept from separating. When one gives undivided attention to the (vital) breath, and brings it to the utmost degree of pliancy, he can become as a (tender) babe. When he has cleansed away the most mysterious sights (of his imagination), he can become without a flaw.

載營魄抱一，能無離乎？專氣致柔，能嬰兒乎？滌除玄覽，能無疵乎？

10. 2. In loving the people and ruling the state, cannot he proceed without any (purpose of) action? In the opening and shutting of his gates of heaven, cannot he do so as a female bird? While his intelligence reaches in every direction, cannot he (appear to) be without knowledge?

愛國治民，能無為乎？天門開闔，能為雌乎？明白四達，能無知乎？

10. 3. (The Tâo) produces (all things) and nourishes them; it produces them and does not claim them as its own; it does all, and yet does not boast of it; it presides over all, and yet does not control them. This is what is called 'The mysterious Quality' (of the Tâo).

生之畜之，生而不有，爲而不恃，長而不宰，
是謂玄德。

CHAPTER 11
虚中章

11.1 The thirty spokes unite in the one nave; but it is on the empty space (for the axle), that the use of the wheel depends. Clay is fashioned into vessels; but it is on their empty hollowness, that their use depends. The door and windows are cut out (from the walls) to form an apartment; but it is on the empty space (within), that its use depends. Therefore, what has a (positive) existence serves for profitable adaptation, and what has not that for (actual) usefulness.

三十輻，共一轂，當其無，有車之用。埏埴以為器，當其無，有器之用。鑿戶牖以為室，當其無，有室之用。故有之以為利，無之以為用。

CHAPTER 12
爲腹章

12. 1. Colour's five hues from th' eyes their sight will take;
Music's five notes the ears as deaf can make;
The flavours five deprive the mouth of taste;
The chariot course, and the wild hunting waste
Make mad the mind; and objects rare and strange,
Sought for, men's conduct will to evil change.
五色令人目盲；五音令人耳聾；五味令人口
爽；馳騁畋獵，令人心發狂；難得之貨，令人
行妨。

12. 2. Therefore the sage seeks to satisfy (the craving of) the belly,
and not the (insatiable longing of the) eyes. He puts from
him the latter, and prefers to seek the former.
是以聖人爲腹不爲目，故去彼取此。

CHAPTER 13
寵辱章

13. 1. Favour and disgrace would seem equally to be feared; honour and great calamity, to be regarded as personal conditions (of the same kind).

寵辱若驚，貴大患若身。

13. 2. What is meant by speaking thus of favour and disgrace? Disgrace is being in a low position (after the enjoyment of favour). The getting that (favour) leads to the apprehension (of losing it), and the losing it leads to the fear of (still greater calamity):—this is what is meant by saying that favour and disgrace would seem equally to be feared.

何謂寵辱若驚？寵爲上，辱爲下，得之若驚，失之若驚，是謂寵辱若驚。

13. 3. And what is meant by saying that honour and great calamity are to be (similarly) regarded as personal conditions? What makes me liable to great calamity is my having the body (which I call myself); if I had not the body, what great calamity could come to me?

何謂貴大患若身？吾所以有大患者，爲吾有身，及吾無身，吾有何患？

13. 3. Therefore he who would administer the kingdom, honouring it as he honours his own person, may be employed to govern it, and he who would administer it with the love which he bears to his own person may be entrusted with it.

故貴以身爲天下，若可寄天下；愛以身爲天下，若可托天下。

CHAPTER 14

道紀章

14. 1. We look at it, and we do not see it, and we name it 'the Equable.' We listen to it, and we do not hear it, and we name it 'the Inaudible.' We try to grasp it, and do not get hold of it, and we name it 'the Subtle.' With these three qualities, it cannot be made the subject of description; and hence we blend them together and obtain The One.

視之不見，名曰夷；聽之不聞，名曰希；搏之不得，名曰微。此三者不可致詰，故混而爲一。

14. 2. Its upper part is not bright, and its lower part is not obscure. Ceaseless in its action, it yet cannot be named, and then it again returns and becomes nothing. This is called the Form of the Formless, and the Semblance of the Invisible; this is called the Fleeting and Indeterminable.

其上不皦，其下不昧。繩繩不可名，復歸于無物。是謂無狀之狀，無物之象，是謂惚恍。

14. 3. We meet it and do not see its Front; we follow it, and do not see its Back. When we can lay hold of the Tâo of old to direct the things of the present day, and are able to know it as it was of old in the beginning, this is called (unwinding) the clue of Tâo.

迎之不見其首，隨之不見其后。執古之道，以禦今之有。舷知古始，是謂道紀。

CHAPTER 15
不盈章

15. 1. The skilful masters (of the Tâo) in old times, with a subtle and exquisite penetration, comprehended its mysteries, and were deep (also) so as to elude men's knowledge. As they were thus beyond men's knowledge, I will make an effort to describe of what sort they appeared to be.

古之善爲道者，微妙玄通，深不可識。夫唯不可識，故強爲之容。

15. 2. Shrinking looked they like those who wade through a stream in winter; irresolute like those who are afraid of all around them; grave like a guest (in awe of his host); evanescent like ice that is melting away; unpretentious like wood that has not been fashioned into anything; vacant like a valley, and dull like muddy water.

豫兮若冬涉川，猶兮若畏四鄰，儼兮其若客，渙兮若冰之將釋，敦兮其若樸，曠兮其若谷，渾兮其若濁。

15. 3. Who can (make) the muddy water (clear)? Let it be still, and it will gradually become clear. Who can secure the condition of rest? Let movement go on, and the condition of rest will gradually arise.

孰能濁以靜之徐清？孰能安以動之徐生？保此道者不欲盈。

15. 4. They who preserve this method of the Tâo do not wish to be full (of themselves). It is through their not being full of themselves that they can afford to seem worn and not appear new and complete.

夫唯不盈，故能蔽而新成。

CHAPTER 16

復命章

16. 1. The (state of) vacancy should be brought to the utmost degree, and that of stillness guarded with unwearying vigour. All things alike go through their processes of activity, and (then) we see them return (to their original state). When things (in the vegetable world) have displayed their luxuriant growth, we see each of them return to its root. This returning to their root is what we call the state of stillness; and that stillness may be called a reporting that they have fulfilled their appointed end.

致虛極，守靜篤。萬物幷作，吾以觀復。夫物蕓蕓，各復歸其根。歸根曰靜，是謂復命。

16. 2. The report of that fulfilment is the regular, unchanging rule. To know that unchanging rule is to be intelligent; not to know it leads to wild movements and evil issues. The knowledge of that unchanging rule produces a (grand) capacity and forbearance, and that capacity and forbearance lead to a community (of feeling with all things). From this community of feeling comes a kingliness of character; and he who is king-like goes on to be heaven-like. In that likeness to heaven he possesses the Tâo. Possessed of the Tâo, he endures long; and to the end of his bodily life, is exempt from all danger of decay.

復命曰常。知常曰明。不知常，妄作凶。知常
容，容乃公，公乃全，全乃天，天乃道，道乃
久。沒身不殆。

CHAPTER 17

我自然章

17. 1. In the highest antiquity, (the people) did not know that there were (their rulers). In the next age they loved them and praised them. In the next they feared them; in the next they despised them. Thus it was that when faith (in the Tâo) was deficient (in the rulers) a want of faith in them ensued (in the people).

太上，不知有之；其次，親而譽之；其次，畏之；其次，侮之。信不足焉，有不信焉。

17. 2. How irresolute did those (earliest rulers) appear, showing (by their reticence) the importance which they set upon their words! Their work was done and their undertakings were successful, while the people all said, 'We are as we are, of ourselves!'

悠兮其貴言。功成，事遂，百姓皆謂：「我自然」。

CHAPTER 18

四有章

18. 1. When the Great Tâo (Way or Method) ceased to be observed, benevolence and righteousness came into vogue. (Then) appeared wisdom and shrewdness, and there ensued great hypocrisy.

大道廢，有仁義；智慧出，有大偽；

18. 2. When harmony no longer prevailed throughout the six kinships, filial sons found their manifestation; when the states and clans fell into disorder, loyal ministers appeared.

六親不和，有孝慈；國家昏亂，有忠臣。

CHAPTER 19

素樸章

19. 1. If we could renounce our sageness and discard our wisdom,
it would be better for the people a hundredfold. If we could
renounce our benevolence and discard our righteousness,
the people would again become filial and kindly. If we could
renounce our artful contrivances and discard our (scheming
for) gain, there would be no thieves nor robbers.

絕聖弃智，民利百倍；絕仁弃義，民復孝慈；
絕巧弃利，盜賊無有。

19. 2. Those three methods (of government)
Thought olden ways in elegance did fail
And made these names their want of worth to veil;
But simple views, and courses plain and true
Would selfish ends and many lusts eschew.

此三者以爲文不足，故令有所屬。見素抱樸，
少私寡欲。

CHAPTER 20
食母章

20. 1. When we renounce learning we have no troubles.
The (ready) 'yes,' and (flattering) 'yea;' —
Small is the difference they display.
But mark their issues, good and ill; —
What space the gulf between shall fill?

絕學無憂。唯之與阿，相去幾何？善之與惡，
相去若何？

What all men fear is indeed to be feared; but how wide
and without end is the range of questions (asking to be
discussed)!

人之所畏，不可不畏。荒兮其未央哉！

20. 2. The multitude of men look satisfied and pleased; as if enjoying a full banquet, as if mounted on a tower in spring. I alone seem listless and still, my desires having as yet given no indication of their presence. I am like an infant which has not yet smiled. I look dejected and forlorn, as if I had no home to go to. The multitude of men all have enough and to spare. I alone seem to have lost everything. My mind is that of a stupid man; I am in a state of chaos.

眾人熙熙，如享太牢，如春登臺。我獨泊兮其未兆，如嬰兒之未孩。儽儽兮若無所歸。眾人皆有余，而我獨若遺。我愚人之心也哉，沌沌兮！

Ordinary men look bright and intelligent, while I alone seem to be benighted. They look full of discrimination, while I alone am dull and confused. I seem to be carried about as on the sea, drifting as if I had nowhere to rest. All men have their spheres of action, while I alone seem dull and incapable, like a rude borderer. (Thus) I alone am different from other men, but I value the nursing-mother (the Tâo).

俗人昭昭，我獨昏昏。俗人察察，我獨悶悶。澹兮其若海，飂兮若無止。眾人皆有以，而我獨頑且鄙。我獨异于人，而貴食母。

CHAPTER 21

從道章

21. 1. The grandest forms of active force
From Tâo come, their only source.
Who can of Tâo the nature tell?
Our sight it flies, our touch as well.
Eluding sight, eluding touch,
The forms of things all in it crouch;
Eluding touch, eluding sight,
There are their semblances, all right.
Profound it is, dark and obscure;
Things' essences all there endure.
Those essences the truth enfold
Of what, when seen, shall then be told.
Now it is so; 'twas so of old.
Its name;—what passes not away;
So, in their beautiful array,
Things form and never know decay.

孔德之容，惟道是從。道之為物，惟恍惟惚。
惚兮恍兮，其中有象；恍兮惚兮，其中有物。
窈兮冥兮，其中有精；其精甚真，其中有信。
自今及古，其名不去，以閱眾甫。

How know I that it is so with all the beauties of existing
things? By this (nature of the Tâo).

吾何以知眾甫之狀哉？ 以此。

CHAPTER 22
抱一章

22. 1. The partial becomes complete; the crooked, straight; the empty, full; the worn out, new. He whose (desires) are few gets them; he whose (desires) are many goes astray.

曲則全，枉則直，窪則盈，敝則新，少則得，多則惑。

22. 2. Therefore the sage holds in his embrace the one thing (of humility), and manifests it to all the world. He is free from self-display, and therefore he shines; from self-assertion, and therefore he is distinguished; from self-boasting, and therefore his merit is acknowledged; from self-complacency, and therefore he acquires superiority. It is because he is thus free from striving that therefore no one in the world is able to strive with him.

是以聖人抱一為天下式。不自見，故明；不自是，故彰；不自伐，故有功；不自矜，故長。

22. 3. That saying of the ancients that 'the partial becomes complete' was not vainly spoken: — all real completion is comprehended under it.

古之所謂曲則全者，豈虛言哉！誠全而歸之。

CHAPTER 23
同道章

23. 1. Abstaining from speech marks him who is obeying the spontaneity of his nature. A violent wind does not last for a whole morning; a sudden rain does not last for the whole day. To whom is it that these (two) things are owing? To Heaven and Earth. If Heaven and Earth cannot make such (spasmodic) actings last long, how much less can man!

希言自然。故飄風不終朝，驟雨不終日。孰為此者？天地。天地尚不能久，而況于人乎？

23. 2. Therefore when one is making the Tâo his business, those who are also pursuing it, agree with him in it, and those who are making the manifestation of its course their object agree with him in that; while even those who are failing in both these things agree with him where they fail.

故從事于道者，同于道；德者，同于德；失者，同于失。

23. 3. Hence, those with whom he agrees as to the Tâo have the happiness of attaining to it; those with whom he agrees as to its manifestation have the happiness of attaining to it; and those with whom he agrees in their failure have also the happiness of attaining (to the Tâo). (But) when there is not faith sufficient (on his part), a want of faith (in him) ensues (on the part of the others).

同于道者，道亦樂得之；同于德者，德亦樂得之；同于失者，失亦樂得之。信不足焉，有不信焉。

CHAPTER 24

不處章

24. 1. He who stands on his tiptoes does not stand firm; he who stretches his legs does not walk (easily). (So), he who displays himself does not shine; he who asserts his own views is not distinguished; he who vaunts himself does not find his merit acknowledged; he who is self-conceited has no superiority allowed to him. Such conditions, viewed from the standpoint of the Tâo, are like remnants of food, or a tumour on the body, which all dislike. Hence those who pursue (the course) of the Tâo do not adopt and allow them.

企者不立，跨者不行。自見者不明，自是者不彰，自伐者無功，自矜者不長。其于道也，曰：餘食贅行。物或惡之，故有道者不處。

CHAPTER 25

混成章

25. 1. There was something undefined and complete, coming into existence before Heaven and Earth. How still it was and formless, standing alone, and undergoing no change, reaching everywhere and in no danger (of being exhausted)! It may be regarded as the Mother of all things.

有物混成，先天地生。寂兮寥兮，獨立而不改，周行而不殆，可以爲天下母。

25. 2. I do not know its name, and I give it the designation of the Tâo (the Way or Course). Making an effort (further) to give it a name I call it The Great.

吾不知其名，字之曰道，強爲之名曰大。

25. 3. Great, it passes on (in constant flow). Passing on, it becomes remote. Having become remote, it returns. Therefore the Tâo is great; Heaven is great; Earth is great; and the (sage) king is also great. In the universe there are four that are great, and the (sage) king is one of them.

大曰逝，逝曰遠，遠曰反。故道大，天大，地大，人亦大。域中有四大，而人居其一焉。

25. 4. Man takes his law from the Earth; the Earth takes its law from Heaven; Heaven takes its law from the Tâo. The law of the Tâo is its being what it is.

人法地，地法天，天法道，道法自然。

CHAPTER 26
輻重章

26. 1. Gravity is the root of lightness; stillness, the ruler of movement.

重為輕根，靜為躁君。

26. 2. Therefore a wise prince, marching the whole day, does not go far from his baggage waggons. Although he may have brilliant prospects to look at, he quietly remains (in his proper place), indifferent to them. How should the lord of a myriad chariots carry himself lightly before the kingdom? If he do act lightly, he has lost his root (of gravity); if he proceed to active movement, he will lose his throne.

是以君子終日行不離輻重，雖有榮觀，燕處超然。奈何萬乘之主，而以身輕天下？輕則失根，躁則失君。

CHAPTER 27

襲明章

27. 1. The skilful traveller leaves no traces of his wheels or footsteps; the skilful speaker says nothing that can be found fault with or blamed; the skilful reckoner uses no tallies; the skilful closer needs no bolts or bars, while to open what he has shut will be impossible; the skilful binder uses no strings or knots, while to unloose what he has bound will be impossible. In the same way the sage is always skilful at saving men, and so he does not cast away any man; he is always skilful at saving things, and so he does not cast away anything. This is called 'Hiding the light of his procedure.'

善行無轍迹，善言無瑕謫，善數不用籌策，善閉無關楗而不可開，善結無繩約而不可解。是以聖人常善救人，故無弃人；常善救物，故無弃物。是謂襲明。

27. 2. Therefore the man of skill is a master (to be looked up to) by him who has not the skill; and he who has not the skill is the helper of (the reputation of) him who has the skill. If the one did not honour his master, and the other did not rejoice in his helper, an (observer), though intelligent, might greatly err about them. This is called 'The utmost degree of mystery.'

故善人者，不善人之師；不善人者，善人之
資。不貴其師，不愛其資，雖智大迷，是謂要
妙。

CHAPTER 28

常德章

28. 1. Who knows his manhood's strength,
    Yet still his female feebleness maintains;
    As to one channel flow the many drains,
    All come to him, yea, all beneath the sky.
    Thus he the constant excellence retains;
    The simple child again, free from all stains.
    知其雄，守其雌，爲天下溪。爲天下溪，常德
    不離，復歸于嬰兒。

    Who knows how white attracts,
    Yet always keeps himself within black's shade,
    The pattern of humility displayed,
    Displayed in view of all beneath the sky;
    He in the unchanging excellence arrayed,
    Endless return to man's first state has made.
    知其白，守其辱，爲天下穀。

Who knows how glory shines,
Yet loves disgrace, nor e'er for it is pale;
Behold his presence in a spacious vale,
To which men come from all beneath the sky.
The unchanging excellence completes its tale;
The simple infant man in him we hail.

為天下穀，常德乃足，復歸于樸。

28. 2. The unwrought material, when divided and distributed,
forms vessels. The sage, when employed, becomes the
Head of all the Officers (of government); and in his greatest
regulations he employs no violent measures.

樸散則為器，聖人用之，則為官長，故大制不
割。

CHAPTER 29
自然章

29. 1. If any one should wish to get the kingdom for himself, and to effect this by what he does, I see that he will not succeed. The kingdom is a spirit-like thing, and cannot be got by active doing. He who would so win it destroys it; he who would hold it in his grasp loses it.

將欲取天下而爲之，吾見其不得已。天下神器，不可爲也，不可執也。爲者敗之，執者失之。

29. 2. The course and nature of things is such that
What was in front is now behind;
What warmed anon we freezing find.
Strength is of weakness oft the spoil;
The store in ruins mocks our toil.

故物或行或隨，或嘘或吹，或强或羸，或載或隳。

Hence the sage puts away excessive effort, extravagance, and easy indulgence.

聖人去甚，去奢，去泰。

CHAPTER 30

不道章

30. 1. He who would assist a lord of men in harmony with the Tâo will not assert his mastery in the kingdom by force of arms. Such a course is sure to meet with its proper return.

以道佐人主者，不以兵強天下。其事好還。

30. 2. Wherever a host is stationed, briars and thorns spring up. In the sequence of great armies there are sure to be bad years.

師之所處，荊棘生焉。大軍之后，必有凶年。

30. 3. A skilful (commander) strikes a decisive blow, and stops. He does not dare (by continuing his operations) to assert and complete his mastery. He will strike the blow, but will be on his guard against being vain or boastful or arrogant in consequence of it. He strikes it as a matter of necessity; he strikes it, but not from a wish for mastery.

善者果而已，不敢以取強。果而勿矜，果而勿伐，果而勿驕。果而不得已，果而勿強。

30. 4. When things have attained their strong maturity they become old. This may be said to be not in accordance with the Tâo: and what is not in accordance with it soon comes to an end.

物壯則老，是謂不道，不道早已。

CHAPTER 31

貴左章

31. 1. Now arms, however beautiful, are instruments of evil omen, hateful, it may be said, to all creatures. Therefore they who have the Tâo do not like to employ them.

夫佳兵者不祥之器，物或惡之，故有道者不處。

31. 2. The superior man ordinarily considers the left hand the most honourable place, but in time of war the right hand. Those sharp weapons are instruments of evil omen, and not the instruments of the superior man; ;—he uses them only on the compulsion of necessity. Calm and repose are what he prizes; victory (by force of arms) is to him undesirable. To consider this desirable would be to delight in the slaughter of men; and he who delights in the slaughter of men cannot get his will in the kingdom.

君子居則貴左，用兵則貴右。兵者不祥之器，非君子之器，不得已而用之，恬淡為上。勝而不美，而美之者，是樂殺人。夫樂殺人者，則不可得志于天下矣。

31. 3. On occasions of festivity to be on the left hand is the prized position; on occasions of mourning, the right hand. The second in command of the army has his place on the left; the general commanding in chief has his on the right;—his place, that is, is assigned to him as in the rites of mourning. He who has killed multitudes of men should weep for them with the bitterest grief; and the victor in battle has his place (rightly) according to those rites.

吉事尚左，凶事尚右。偏將軍居左，上將軍居右。言以喪禮處之。殺人之衆，以悲哀泣之，戰勝以喪禮處之。

CHAPTER 32

知止章

32. 1. The Tâo, considered as unchanging, has no name.

道常無名，

32. 2. Though in its primordial simplicity it may be small, the whole world dares not deal with (one embodying) it as a minister. If a feudal prince or the king could guard and hold it, all would spontaneously submit themselves to him.

樸，雖小，天下莫能臣也。侯王若能守之，萬物將自賓。

32. 3. Heaven and Earth (under its guidance) unite together and send down the sweet dew, which, without the directions of men, reaches equally everywhere as of its own accord.

天地相合，以降甘露，民莫之令而自均。

32. 4. As soon as it proceeds to action, it has a name. When it once has that name, (men) can know to rest in it. When they know to rest in it, they can be free from all risk of failure and error.

始制有名，名亦既有，夫亦將知止，知止可以不殆。

32. 5. The relation of the Tâo to all the world is like that of the great rivers and seas to the streams from the valleys.

譬道之在天下，猶川穀之于江海。

CHAPTER 33
盡己章

33. 1. He who knows other men is discerning; he who knows himself is intelligent. He who overcomes others is strong; he who overcomes himself is mighty. He who is satisfied with his lot is rich; he who goes on acting with energy has a (firm) will.

知人者智，自知者明。勝人者有力，自勝者強。知足者富。強行者有志。

33. 2. He who does not fail in the requirements of his position, continues long; he who dies and yet does not perish, has longevity.

不失其所者久。死而不亡者壽。

CHAPTER 34

成大章

34. 1. All-pervading is the Great Tâo! It may be found on the left hand and on the right.

大道泛兮，其可左右。

34. 2. All things depend on it for their production, which it gives to them, not one refusing obedience to it. When its work is accomplished, it does not claim the name of having done it. It clothes all things as with a garment, and makes no assumption of being their lord;—it may be named in the smallest things. All things return (to their root and disappear), and do not know that it is it which presides over their doing so;—it may be named in the greatest things.

萬物恃之而生而不辭，功成而不有，衣養萬物而不爲主。常無欲，可名于小；萬物歸焉而不爲主，可名爲大。

34. 3. Hence the sage is able (in the same way) to accomplish his great achievements. It is through his not making himself great that he can accomplish them.

以其終不自爲大，故能成其大。

CHAPTER 35

大象章

35. 1. To him who holds in his hands the Great Image (of the invisible Tao), the whole world repairs. Men resort to him, and receive no hurt, but (find) rest, peace, and the feeling of ease.

執大象，天下注。注而不害，安平太。

35. 2. Music and dainties will make the passing guest stop (for a time). But though the Tâo as it comes from the mouth, seems insipid and has no flavour, though it seems not worth being looked at or listened to, the use of it is inexhaustible.

樂與餌，過客止。道之出口，淡乎其無味，視之不足見，聽之不足聞，用之不足既。

CHAPTER 36

微明章

36. 1. When one is about to take an inspiration, he is sure to make a (previous) expiration; when he is going to weaken another, he will first strengthen him; when he is going to overthrow another, he will first have raised him up; when he is going to despoil another, he will first have made gifts to him: — this is called 'Hiding the light (of his procedure).'

將欲歙之，必固張之。將欲弱之，必固強之。
將欲廢之，必固舉之。將欲奪之，必固與之。
是謂微明。

36. 2. The soft overcomes the hard; and the weak the strong.

柔弱勝剛強。

36. 3. Fishes should not be taken from the deep; instruments for the profit of a state should not be shown to the people.

魚不可脫于淵，國之利器不可以示人。

CHAPTER 37

無爲章

37. 1. The Tâo in its regular course does nothing (for the sake of doing it), and so there is nothing which it does not do.
道常無爲而無不爲，

37. 2. If princes and kings were able to maintain it, all things would of themselves be transformed by them.
侯王若骵守之，萬物將自化。

37. 3. If this transformation became to me an object of desire, I would express the desire by the nameless simplicity.
化而欲作，吾將鎮之以無名之樸。

Simplicity without a name
Is free from all external aim.
With no desire, at rest and still,
All things go right as of their will.
無名之樸，夫亦將無欲。不欲以靜，天下將自
定。

PART II

CHAPTER 38

處厚章

38. 1. (Those who) possessed in highest degree the attributes (of the Tao) did not (seek) to show them, and therefore they possessed them (in fullest measure). (Those who) possessed in a lower degree those attributes (sought how) not to lose them, and therefore they did not possess them (in fullest measure).

上德不德，是以有德；下德不失德，是以無德。

38. 2. (Those who) possessed in the highest degree those attributes did nothing (with a purpose), and had no need to do anything. (Those who) possessed them in a lower degree were (always) doing, and had need to be so doing.

上德無爲而無以爲；下德無爲而有以爲。

38. 3. (Those who) possessed the highest benevolence were (always seeking) to carry it out, and had no need to be doing so. (Those who) possessed the highest righteousness were (always seeking) to carry it out, and had need to be so doing.

上仁爲之而無以爲；上義爲之而有以爲。

38. 4. (Those who) possessed the highest (sense of) propriety were (always seeking) to show it, and when men did not respond to it, they bared the arm and marched up to them.

上禮爲之而莫之應，則攘臂而扔之。

38. 5. Thus it was that when the Tâo was lost, its attributes appeared; when its attributes were lost, benevolence appeared; when benevolence was lost, righteousness appeared; and when righteousness was lost, the proprieties appeared.

故失道而后德，失德而后仁，失仁而后義，失義而后禮，

38. 6. Now propriety is the attenuated form of leal-heartedness and good faith, and is also the commencement of disorder; swift apprehension is (only) a flower of the Tâo, and is the beginning of stupidity.

夫禮者忠信之薄，而亂之首。前識者，道之華，萬愚之始。

38. 7. Thus it is that the Great man abides by what is solid, and eschews what is flimsy; dwells with the fruit and not with the flower. It is thus that he puts away the one and makes choice of the other.

是以大丈夫處其厚，不居其薄，處其實，不居其華。故去彼取此。

CHAPTER 39

得一章

39. 1. The things which from of old have got the One (the Tâo)
are —

昔之得一者，

Heaven which by it is bright and pure;
Earth rendered thereby firm and sure;
Spirits with powers by it supplied;
Valleys kept full throughout their void
All creatures which through it do live
Princes and kings who from it get
The model which to all they give.

天得一以清，地得一以寧，神得一以靈，穀一
以盈，萬物得一以生，侯王得一以為天下貞。

All these are the results of the One (Tao).

其致之。

39. 2. If heaven were not thus pure, it soon would rend;
If earth were not thus sure, 'twould break and bend;
Without these powers, the spirits soon would fail;
If not so filled, the drought would parch each vale;
Without that life, creatures would pass away;
Princes and kings, without that moral sway,
However grand and high, would all decay.

天無以清將恐裂，地無以寧將恐發，神無以靈
將恐歇，穀無以盈將恐竭，萬物無以生將恐
滅，侯王無以貴高將恐 蹶。

39. 3. Thus it is that dignity finds its (firm) root in its (previous) meanness, and what is lofty finds its stability in the lowness (from which it rises). Hence princes and kings call themselves 'Orphans,' 'Men of small virtue,' and as 'Carriages without a nave.' Is not this an acknowledgment that in their considering themselves mean they see the foundation of their dignity? So it is that in the enumeration of the different parts of a carriage we do not come on what makes it answer the ends of a carriage. They do not wish to show themselves elegant-looking as jade, but (prefer) to be coarse-looking as an (ordinary) stone.

故貴以賤為本，高以下為基。是以侯王自謂
孤、寡、不穀，此非以賤為本邪？非歟？故至
譽無譽。不欲琭琭如玉，珞珞如石。

CHAPTER 40
反弱章

40. 1. The movement of the Tâo
By contraries proceeds;
And weakness marks the course
Of Tâo's mighty deeds.
反者道之動；弱者道之用。

40. 2. All things under heaven sprang from It as existing (and named); that existence sprang from It as non-existent (and not named).
天下萬物生于有，有生于無。

CHAPTER 41

聞道章

41. 1. Scholars of the highest class, when they hear about the Tâo, earnestly carry it into practice. Scholars of the middle class, when they have heard about it, seem now to keep it and now to lose it. Scholars of the lowest class, when they have heard about it, laugh greatly at it. If it were not (thus) laughed at, it would not be fit to be the Tâo.

上士聞道，勤而行之；中士聞道，若存若亡；
下士聞道，大笑之。不笑不足以爲道。

41. 2. Therefore the sentence-makers have thus expressed themselves:—

故建言有之：

'The Tâo, when brightest seen, seems light to lack;
Who progress in it makes, seems drawing back;
Its even way is like a rugged track.
Its highest virtue from the vale doth rise;
Its greatest beauty seems to offend the eyes;
And he has most whose lot the least supplies.
Its firmest virtue seems but poor and low;
Its solid truth seems change to undergo;
Its largest square doth yet no corner show
A vessel great, it is the slowest made;
Loud is its sound, but never word it said;
A semblance great, the shadow of a shade.'

明道若昧，進道若退，夷道若纇，上德若谷，
大白若辱，廣德若不足，建德若偷，質德若
渝，大方無隅，大器晚成，大音希聲，大象無
形，

41. 3. The Tâo is hidden, and has no name; but it is the Tâo which
is skilful at imparting (to all things what they need) and
making them complete.

道隱無名。夫唯道，善貸且成。

CHAPTER 42
沖和章

42. 1. The Tâo produced One; One produced Two; Two produced Three; Three produced All things. All things leave behind them the Obscurity (out of which they have come), and go forward to embrace the Brightness (into which they have emerged), while they are harmonised by the Breath of Vacancy.

道生一，一生二，二生三，三生萬物。萬物負陰而抱陽，衝氣以為和。

42. 2. What men dislike is to be orphans, to have little virtue, to be as carriages without naves; and yet these are the designations which kings and princes use for themselves. So it is that some things are increased by being diminished, and others are diminished by being increased.

人之所惡，唯孤、寡、不穀，而王公以為稱。故物或損之而益，或益之而損。

42. 3. What other men (thus) teach, I also teach. The violent and strong do not die their natural death. I will make this the basis of my teaching.

人之所教，我亦教之，強梁者不得其死，吾將以為教父。

CHAPTER 43
至柔章

43. 1. The softest thing in the world dashes against and overcomes the hardest; that which has no (substantial) existence enters where there is no crevice. I know hereby what advantage belongs to doing nothing (with a purpose).

天下之至柔，馳騁天下之至堅，無有入無間。
吾是以知無為之有益。

43. 2. There are few in the world who attain to the teaching without words, and the advantage arising from non-action.

不言之教，無為之益，天下希及之。

CHAPTER 44

知止章

44. 1. Or fame or life,
   Which do you hold more dear?
   Or life or wealth,
   To which would you adhere?
   Keep life and lose those other things;
   Keep them and lose your life: — which brings
   Sorrow and pain more near?
   名與身孰親？身與貨孰多？得與亡孰病？

44. 2. Thus we may see,
   Who cleaves to fame
   Rejects what is more great;
   Who loves large stores
   Gives up the richer state.
   是故甚愛必大費，多藏必厚亡。

44. 3. Who is content
Needs fear no shame.
Who knows to stop
Incurs no blame.
From danger free
Long live shall he.
知足不辱，知止不殆，可以長久。

CHAPTER 45
清靜章

45. 1. Who thinks his great achievements poor
Shall find his vigour long endure.
Of greatest fulness, deemed a void,
Exhaustion ne'er shall stem the tide.
Do thou what's straight still crooked deem;
Thy greatest art still stupid seem,
And eloquence a stammering scream.

大成若缺，其用不弊；大盈若衝，其用不窮。
大直若屈，大巧若拙，大辯若訥。

45. 2. Constant action overcomes cold; being still overcomes heat.
Purity and stillness give the correct law to all under heaven.

靜勝躁，寒勝熱，清靜爲天下正。

CHAPTER 46

知足章

46. 1. When the Tâo prevails in the world, they send back their swift horses to (draw) the dung-carts. When the Tâo is disregarded in the world, the war-horses breed in the border lands.

天下有道，却走馬以糞；天下無道，戎馬生于郊。

46. 2. There is no guilt greater than to sanction ambition; no calamity greater than to be discontented with one's lot; no fault greater than the wish to be getting. Therefore the sufficiency of contentment is an enduring and unchanging sufficiency.

禍莫大于不知足；咎莫大于欲得。故知足之足，常足矣。

CHAPTER 47
天道章

47. 1. Without going outside his door, one understands (all that takes place) under the sky; without looking out from his window, one sees the Tâo of Heaven. The farther that one goes out (from himself), the less he knows.

不出戶，知天下；不窺牖，見天道。其出彌遠，其知彌少。

47. 2. Therefore the sages got their knowledge without travelling; gave their (right) names to things without seeing them; and accomplished their ends without any purpose of doing so.

是以聖人不行而知，不見而名，無為而成。

CHAPTER 48
日損章

48. 1. He who devotes himself to learning (seeks) from day to day to increase (his knowledge); he who devotes himself to the Tâo (seeks) from day to day to diminish (his doing).

為學日益，為道日損。

48. 2. He diminishes it and again diminishes it, till he arrives at doing nothing (on purpose). Having arrived at this point of non-action, there is nothing which he does not do.

損之又損，以至于無為。無為而無不為。

48. 3. He who gets as his own all under heaven does so by giving himself no trouble (with that end). If one take trouble (with that end), he is not equal to getting as his own all under heaven.

取天下常以無事，及其有事，不足以取天下。

CHAPTER 49

德善章

49. 1. The sage has no invariable mind of his own; he makes the mind of the people his mind.

聖人無常心，以百姓心為心。

49. 2. To those who are good (to me), I am good; and to those who are not good (to me), I am also good; — and thus (all) get to be good. To those who are sincere (with me), I am sincere; and to those who are not sincere (with me), I am also sincere; — and thus (all) get to be sincere.

善者吾善之，不善者吾亦善之，德善。信者吾信之，不信者吾亦信之，德信。

49. 3. The sage has in the world an appearance of indecision, and keeps his mind in a state of indifference to all. The people all keep their eyes and ears directed to him, and he deals with them all as his children.

聖人在天下，歙歙焉；為天下，渾其心。百姓皆注其耳目，聖人皆孩之。

CHAPTER 50

生死章

50. 1. Men come forth and live; they enter (again) and die.

出生入死。

50. 2. Of every ten three are ministers of life (to themselves); and three are ministers of death.

生之徒十有三，死之徒十有三，

50. 3. There are also three in every ten whose aim is to live, but whose movements tend to the land (or place) of death. And for what reason? Because of their excessive endeavours to perpetuate life.

人之生，動之死地，亦十有三。夫何故？以其生生之厚。

50. 4. But I have heard that he who is skilful in managing the life entrusted to him for a time travels on the land without having to shun rhinoceros or tiger, and enters a host without having to avoid buff coat or sharp weapon. The rhinoceros finds no place in him into which to thrust its horn, nor the tiger a place in which to fix its claws, nor the weapon a place to admit its point. And for what reason? Because there is in him no place of death.

蓋聞善攝生者，陸行不遇兕虎，入軍不被兵甲。兕無所投其角，虎無所措其爪，兵無所容其刃，夫何故？以其無死地。

CHAPTER 51

尊貴章

51. 1. All things are produced by the Tâo, and nourished by its outflowing operation. They receive their forms according to the nature of each, and are completed according to the circumstances of their condition. Therefore all things without exception honour the Tâo, and exalt its outflowing operation.

道生之，德畜之，物形之，勢成之。是以萬物莫不尊道而貴德。

51. 2. This honouring of the Tâo and exalting of its operation is not the result of any ordination, but always a spontaneous tribute.

道之尊，德之貴，夫莫之命而常自然。

51. 3. Thus it is that the Tâo produces (all things), nourishes them, brings them to their full growth, nurses them, completes them, matures them, maintains them, and overspreads them.

故道生之，德畜之，長之育之，亭之毒之，養之覆之。

51. 4. It produces them and makes no claim to the possession of them; it carries them through their processes and does not vaunt its ability in doing so; it brings them to maturity and exercises no control over them; — this is called its mysterious operation.

生而不有，爲而不恃，長而不宰。是謂玄德。

CHAPTER 52

守母章

52. 1. (The Tâo) which originated all under the sky is to be considered as the mother of them all.

天下有始，以為天下母。

52. 2. When the mother is found, we know what her children should be. When one knows that he is his mother's child, and proceeds to guard (the qualities of) the mother that belong to him, to the end of his life he will be free from all peril.

既得其母，以知其子；既知其子，復守其母，
沒身不殆。

52. 3. Let him keep his mouth closed, and shut up the portals (of his nostrils), and all his life he will be exempt from laborious exertion. Let him keep his mouth open, and (spend his breath) in the promotion of his affairs, and all his life there will be no safety for him.

塞其兌，閉其門，終身不勤；開其兌，濟其
身不救。

52. 4. The perception of what is small is (the secret of clear-sightedness; the guarding of what is soft and tender is (the secret of) strength.

見小曰明，守柔曰強。

52. 5. Who uses well his light,
Reverting to its (source so) bright,
Will from his body ward all blight,
And hides the unchanging from men's sight.

用其光，復歸其明，無遺身殃。是為習常。

CHAPTER 53
大道章

53. 1. If I were suddenly to become known, and (put into a position to) conduct (a government) according to the Great Tâo, what I should be most afraid of would be a boastful display.
使我介然有知，行于大道，惟施是畏。

53. 2. The great Tâo (or way) is very level and easy; but people love the by-ways.
大道甚夷，而民好逕。

53. 3. Their court(-yards and buildings) shall be well kept, but their fields shall be ill-cultivated, and their granaries very empty. They shall wear elegant and ornamented robes, carry a sharp sword at their girdle, pamper themselves in eating and drinking, and have a superabundance of property and wealth;—such (princes) may be called robbers and boasters. This is contrary to the Tâo surely!
朝甚除，田甚蕪，倉甚虛；服文彩，帶利劍，厭飲食，財貨有余，是謂盜誇。非道也哉！

CHAPTER 54

善建章

54. 1. What (Tao's) skilful planter plants
Can never be uptorn;
What his skilful arms enfold,
From him can ne'er be borne.
Sons shall bring in lengthening line,
Sacrifices to his shrine.
善建者不拔，善抱者不脫，子孫以祭祀不輟。

54. 2. Tâo when nursed within one's self,
His vigour will make true;
And where the family it rules
What riches will accrue!
The neighbourhood where it prevails
In thriving will abound;
And when 'tis seen throughout the state,
Good fortune will be found.
Employ it the kingdom o'er,
And men thrive all around.
修之于身，其德乃眞；修之于家，其德乃余；
修之于鄉，其德乃長；修之于邦其德乃豐；修
之于天下，其德乃普。

54. 3. In this way the effect will be seen in the person, by the observation of different cases; in the family; in the neighbourhood; in the state; and in the kingdom.

故以身觀身，以家觀家，以鄉觀鄉，以邦觀邦，以天下觀天下。

54. 4. How do I know that this effect is sure to hold thus all under the sky? By this (method of observation).

吾何以知天下然哉？以此。

CHAPTER 55

含德章

55. 1. He who has in himself abundantly the attributes (of the Tâo) is like an infant. Poisonous insects will not sting him; fierce beasts will not seize him; birds of prey will not strike him.
含德之厚，比于赤子。毒蟲不螫，猛獸不據，攫鳥不搏。

55. 2. (The infant's) bones are weak and its sinews soft, but yet its grasp is firm. It knows not yet the union of male and female, and yet its virile member may be excited;—showing the perfection of its physical essence. All day long it will cry without its throat becoming hoarse;—showing the harmony (in its constitution).
骨弱筋柔而握固，未知牝牡之合而朘作，精之至也。終日號而不嗄，和之至也。

55. 3. To him by whom this harmony is known,
      (The secret of) the unchanging (Tao) is shown,
      And in the knowledge wisdom finds its throne.
      All life-increasing arts to evil turn;
      Where the mind makes the vital breath to burn,
      (False) is the strength, (and o'er it we should mourn.)

知和曰常，知常曰明。益生曰祥。心使氣曰強。

55. 4. When things have become strong, they (then) become old, which may be said to be contrary to the Tâo. Whatever is contrary to the Tâo soon ends.

物壯則老，是謂不道，不道早已。

CHAPTER 56

道貴章

56. 1. He who knows (the Tâo) does not (care to) speak (about it); he who is (ever ready to) speak about it does not know it.

知者不言，言者不知。

56. 2. He (who knows it) will keep his mouth shut and close the portals (of his nostrils). He will blunt his sharp points and unravel the complications of things; he will attemper his brightness, and bring himself into agreement with the obscurity (of others). This is called 'the Mysterious Agreement.'

塞其兌，閉其門，挫其銳，解其紛，和其光，同其塵。是謂玄同。

56. 3. (Such an one) cannot be treated familiarly or distantly; he is beyond all consideration of profit or injury; of nobility or meanness:—he is the noblest man under heaven.

故不可得而親，不可得而疏；不可得而利，不可得而害；不可得而貴，不可得而賤。故為天下貴。

CHAPTER 57

治國章

57. 1. A state may be ruled by (measures of) correction; weapons of war may be used with crafty dexterity; (but) the kingdom is made one's own (only) by freedom from action and purpose.

以正治國，以奇用兵，以無事取天下。

57. 2. How do I know that it is so? By these facts:—In the kingdom the multiplication of prohibitive enactments increases the poverty of the people; the more implements to add to their profit that the people have, the greater disorder is there in the state and clan; the more acts of crafty dexterity that men possess, the more do strange contrivances appear; the more display there is of legislation, the more thieves and robbers there are.

吾何以知其然哉？以此。天下多忌諱，而民彌貧；朝多利器，國家滋昏；人多伎巧，奇物滋起；法令滋彰，盜賊多有。

57. 3. Therefore a sage has said, 'I will do nothing (of purpose), and the people will be transformed of themselves; I will be fond of keeping still, and the people will of themselves become correct. I will take no trouble about it, and the people will of themselves become rich; I will manifest no ambition, and the people will of themselves attain to the primitive simplicity.'

故聖人雲：我無爲而民自化，我好靜而民自正，我無事而民自富，我無欲而民自樸。

CHAPTER 58

察政章

58. 1. The government that seems the most unwise,
Oft goodness to the people best supplies;
That which is meddling, touching everything,
Will work but ill, and disappointment bring.

其政悶悶，其民淳淳；其政察察，其民缺缺。

Misery!—happiness is to be found by its side! Happiness!—
misery lurks beneath it! Who knows what either will come
to in the end?

禍兮福之所倚，福兮禍之所伏。孰知其極？

58. 2. Shall we then dispense with correction? The (method of)
correction shall by a turn become distortion, and the good in
it shall by a turn become evil. The delusion of the people (on
this point) has indeed subsisted for a long time.

其無正。正復為奇，善復為妖。人之迷，其日
固久。

58. 3. Therefore the sage is (like) a square which cuts no one (with its angles); (like) a corner which injures no one (with its sharpness). He is straightforward, but allows himself no license; he is bright, but does not dazzle.

是以聖人方而不割，廉而不劌，眞而不肆，光而不耀。

CHAPTER 59

長生章

59. 1. For regulating the human (in our constitution) and rendering the (proper) service to the heavenly, there is nothing like moderation.

治人，事天，莫若嗇。

59. 2. It is only by this moderation that there is effected an early return (to man's normal state). That early return is what I call the repeated accumulation of the attributes (of the Tâo). With that repeated accumulation of those attributes, there comes the subjugation (of every obstacle to such return). Of this subjugation we know not what shall be the limit; and when one knows not what the limit shall be, he may be the ruler of a state.

夫唯嗇，是以早服；早服謂之重積德；重積德
則爲不克；無不克則莫知其極；莫知其極，可
以有國；

59. 3. He who possesses the mother of the state may continue long. His case is like that (of the plant) of which we say that its roots are deep and its flower stalks firm: — this is the way to secure that its enduring life shall long be seen.

有國之母，可以長久。是謂深根固柢，長生久視之道。

CHAPTER 60
治大國章

60. 1. Governing a great state is like cooking small fish.
治大國，若烹小鮮。

60. 2. Let the kingdom be governed according to the Tâo, and the manes of the departed will not manifest their spiritual energy. It is not that those manes have not that spiritual energy, but it will not be employed to hurt men. It is not that it could not hurt men, but neither does the ruling sage hurt them.
以道莅天下，其鬼不神；非其鬼不神，其神不傷人，非其神不傷人，聖人亦不傷人。

60. 3. When these two do not injuriously affect each other, their good influences converge in the virtue (of the Tâo).
夫兩不相傷，故德交歸焉。

CHAPTER 61

写下章

61. 1. What makes a great state is its being (like) a low-lying, down-flowing (stream);—it becomes the centre to which tend (all the small states) under heaven.

大國者下流，天下之交。

61. 2. (To illustrate from) the case of all females:—the female always overcomes the male by her stillness. Stillness may be considered (a sort of) abasement.

天下之牝，牝常以靜勝牡，以靜爲下。

61. 3. Thus it is that a great state, by condescending to small states, gains them for itself; and that small states, by abasing themselves to a great state, win it over to them. In the one case the abasement leads to gaining adherents, in the other case to procuring favour.

故大國以下小國，則取小國；小國以下大國，則取大國。故或下以取，或下而取。

61. 4. The great state only wishes to unite men together and nourish them; a small state only wishes to be received by, and to serve, the other. Each gets what it desires, but the great state must learn to abase itself.

大國不過欲兼畜人，小國不過欲入事人。夫兩者各得所欲，大者宜爲下。

CHAPTER 62

道奧章

62. 1. Tâo has of all things the most honoured place.
No treasures give good men so rich a grace;
Bad men it guards, and doth their ill efface.

道者萬物之奧。善人之寶，不善人之所保。

62. 2. (Its) admirable words can purchase honour; (its) admirable
deeds can raise their performer above others. Even men who
are not good are not abandoned by it.

美言可以示尊，美行可以加人。人之不善，何
弃之有？

62. 3. Therefore when the sovereign occupies his place as the Son
of Heaven, and he has appointed his three ducal ministers,
though (a prince) were to send in a round symbol-of-rank
large enough to fill both the hands, and that as the precursor
of the team of horses (in the court-yard), such an offering
would not be equal to (a lesson of) this Tâo, which one might
present on his knees.

故立天下，置三公，雖有拱璧以先駟馬，不如
坐進此道。

62. 4. Why was it that the ancients prized this Tâo so much? Was it not because it could be got by seeking for it, and the guilty could escape (from the stain of their guilt) by it? This is the reason why all under heaven consider it the most valuable thing.

古之所以貴此道者何？不曰：求以得，有罪以免邪？故為天下貴。

CHAPTER 63

無難章

63. 1. (It is the way of the Tâo) to act without (thinking of) acting; to conduct affairs without (feeling the) trouble of them; to taste without discerning any flavour; to consider what is small as great, and a few as many; and to recompense injury with kindness.

爲無爲，事無事，味無味。大小多小，報怨以德。

63. 2. (The master of it) anticipates things that are difficult while they are easy, and does things that would become great while they are small. All difficult things in the world are sure to arise from a previous state in which they were easy, and all great things from one in which they were small. Therefore the sage, while he never does what is great, is able on that account to accomplish the greatest things.

圖難于其易，爲大于其細。天下難事，必作于易；天下大事，必作于細。是以聖人終不無大，故能成其大。

63. 3. He who lightly promises is sure to keep but little faith; he who is continually thinking things easy is sure to find them difficult. Therefore the sage sees difficulty even in what seems easy, and so never has any difficulties.

夫輕諾必寡信，多易必多難。是以聖人猶難之，故終無難矣。

CHAPTER 64

輔物章

64. 1. That which is at rest is easily kept hold of; before a thing has given indications of its presence, it is easy to take measures against it; that which is brittle is easily broken; that which is very small is easily dispersed. Action should be taken before a thing has made its appearance; order should be secured before disorder has begun.

其安易持，其未兆易謀，其脆易泮，其微易散。爲之于未有，治之于未亂。

64. 2. The tree which fills the arms grew from the tiniest sprout; the tower of nine storeys rose from a (small) heap of earth; the journey of a thousand li commenced with a single step.

合抱之木，生于毫末；九層之臺，起于累土；千裏之行，始于足下。

64. 3. He who acts (with an ulterior purpose) does harm; he who takes hold of a thing (in the same way) loses his hold. The sage does not act (so), and therefore does no harm; he does not lay hold (so), and therefore does not lose his bold. (But) people in their conduct of affairs are constantly ruining them when they are on the eve of success. If they were careful at the end, as (they should be) at the beginning, they would not so ruin them.

為者敗之，執者失之。是以聖人無為故無敗，無執故無失。民之從事，常于幾成而敗之。慎終如始，則無敗事。

64. 4. Therefore the sage desires what (other men) do not desire, and does not prize things difficult to get; he learns what (other men) do not learn, and turns back to what the multitude of men have passed by. Thus he helps the natural development of all things, and does not dare to act (with an ulterior purpose of his own).

是以聖人欲不欲，不貴難得之貨；學不學，復衆人之所過。以輔萬物之自然，而不敢為。

CHAPTER 65

玄德章

65. 1. The ancients who showed their skill in practising the Tâo did so, not to enlighten the people, but rather to make them simple and ignorant.

古之善爲道者，非以明民，將以愚之。

65. 2. The difficulty in governing the people arises from their having much knowledge. He who (tries to) govern a state by his wisdom is a scourge to it; while he who does not (try to) do so is a blessing.

民之難治，以其智多。故以智治國，國之賊；
不以智治國，國之福。

65. 3. He who knows these two things finds in them also his model and rule. Ability to know this model and rule constitutes what we call the mysterious excellence (of a governor). Deep and far-reaching is such mysterious excellence, showing indeed its possessor as opposite to others, but leading them to a great conformity to him.

知此兩者亦稽式。常知稽式，是謂玄德。玄德
深矣遠矣；與物反矣！然后乃至大順。

CHAPTER 66

江海章

66. 1. That whereby the rivers and seas are able to receive the homage and tribute of all the valley streams, is their skill in being lower than they;—it is thus that they are the kings of them all. So it is that the sage (ruler), wishing to be above men, puts himself by his words below them, and, wishing to be before them, places his person behind them.

江海所以能爲百穀王者，以其善下之，故能爲百穀王。是以聖人欲上民，必以言下之；欲先民，必以身后之。

66. 2. In this way though he has his place above them, men do not feel his weight, nor though he has his place before them, do they feel it an injury to them.

是以聖人處上而民不重；處前而民不害。

66. 3. Therefore all in the world delight to exalt him and do not weary of him. Because he does not strive, no one finds it possible to strive with him.

是以天下樂推而不厭。以其不爭，故天下莫能與之爭。

CHAPTER 67

三寶章

67. 1. All the world says that, while my Tâo is great, it yet appears to be inferior (to other systems of teaching). Now it is just its greatness that makes it seem to be inferior. If it were like any other (system), for long would its smallness have been known!

天下皆謂我道大，似不肖。夫唯大，故似不肖。若肖，久矣其細也夫。

67. 2. But I have three precious things which I prize and hold fast. The first is gentleness; the second is economy; and the third is shrinking from taking precedence of others.

我有三寶，持而保之。一曰慈，二曰儉，三曰不敢爲天下先。

67. 3. With that gentleness I can be bold; with that economy I can be liberal; shrinking from taking precedence of others, I can become a vessel of the highest honour. Now-a-days they give up gentleness and are all for being bold; economy, and are all for being liberal; the hindmost place, and seek only to be foremost; — (of all which the end is) death.

慈故能勇，儉故能廣，不敢為天下先，故能成器長。今舍慈且勇，舍儉且廣，舍后且先，死矣！

67. 4. Gentleness is sure to be victorious even in battle, and firmly to maintain its ground. Heaven will save its possessor, by his (very) gentleness protecting him.

夫慈，以戰則勝，以守則固。天將救之，以慈衛之。

CHAPTER 68
不爭章

68. 1. He who in (Tao's) wars has skill Assumes no martial port;
He who fights with most good will
To rage makes no resort.
He who vanquishes yet still
Keeps from his foes apart;
He whose hests men most fulfil
Yet humbly plies his art.

善為士者不武，善戰者不怒，善勝敵者不與，
善用人者為之下。

Thus we say, 'He ne'er contends,
And therein is his might.'
Thus we say, 'Men's wills he bends,
That they with him unite.'
Thus we say, 'Like Heaven's his ends,
No sage of old more bright.'

是謂不爭之德，是謂用人之力，是謂配天之
極。

CHAPTER 69

用兵章

69. 1. A master of the art of war has said, 'I do not dare to be the host (to commence the war); I prefer to be the guest (to act on the defensive). I do not dare to advance an inch; I prefer to retire a foot.' This is called marshalling the ranks where there are no ranks; baring the arms (to fight) where there are no arms to bare; grasping the weapon where there is no weapon to grasp; advancing against the enemy where there is no enemy.

用兵有言：「吾不敢為主而為客，不敢進寸而退尺。」是謂行無行，攘無臂，執無兵，扔無敵。

69. 2. There is no calamity greater than lightly engaging in war. To do that is near losing (the gentleness) which is so precious. Thus it is that when opposing weapons are (actually) crossed, he who deplores (the situation) conquers.

禍莫大于輕敵，輕敵幾喪吾寶。故抗兵相加，哀者勝矣。

CHAPTER 70

懷玉章

70. 1. My words are very easy to know, and very easy to practise; but there is no one in the world who is able to know and able to practise them.

吾言甚易知，甚易行。天下莫能知，莫能行。

70. 2. There is an originating and all-comprehending (principle) in my words, and an authoritative law for the things (which I enforce). It is because they do not know these, that men do not know me.

言有宗，事有君。夫唯無知，是以不我知。

70. 3. They who know me are few, and I am on that account (the more) to be prized. It is thus that the sage wears (a poor garb of) hair cloth, while he carries his (signet of) jade in his bosom.

知我者希，則我者貴。是以聖人被褐懷玉。

CHAPTER 71

不病章

71. 1. To know and yet (think) we do not know is the highest (attainment); not to know (and yet think) we do know is a disease.

知，不知，上；不知，知，病。

71. 2. It is simply by being pained at (the thought of) having this disease that we are preserved from it. The sage has not the disease. He knows the pain that would be inseparable from it, and therefore he does not have it.

聖人不病，以其病病。夫唯病病，是以不病。

CHAPTER 72

畏威章

72. 1. When the people do not fear what they ought to fear, that which is their great dread will come on them.

民不畏威，則大威至。

72. 2. Let them not thoughtlessly indulge themselves in their ordinary life; let them not act as if weary of what that life depends on.

無狎其所居，無厭其所生。

72. 3. It is by avoiding such indulgence that such weariness does not arise.

夫唯不厭，是以不厭。

72. 4. Therefore the sage knows (these things) of himself, but does not parade (his knowledge); loves, but does not (appear to set a) value on, himself. And thus he puts the latter alternative away and makes choice of the former.

是以聖人自知不自見，自愛不自貴。故去彼取此。

CHAPTER 73
天網章

73. 1. He whose boldness appears in his daring (to do wrong, in defiance of the laws) is put to death; he whose boldness appears in his not daring (to do so) lives on. Of these two cases the one appears to be advantageous, and the other to be injurious. But

When Heaven's anger smites a man,
Who the cause shall truly scan?

On this account the sage feels a difficulty (as to what to do in the former case).
勇于敢則殺，勇于不敢則活。此兩者，或利或害，天之所惡，孰知其故？是以聖人猶難之。

73. 2. It is the way of Heaven not to strive, and yet it skilfully overcomes; not to speak, and yet it is skilful in (obtaining a reply; does not call, and yet men come to it of themselves. Its demonstrations are quiet, and yet its plans are skilful and effective. The meshes of the net of Heaven are large; far apart, but letting nothing escape.
天之道，不爭而善勝，不言而善應，不召而自來，然而善謀。天網恢恢，疏而不失。

CHAPTER 74
司殺章

74. 1. The people do not fear death; to what purpose is it to (try to) frighten them with death? If the people were always in awe of death, and I could always seize those who do wrong, and put them to death, who would dare to do wrong?

民不畏死，奈何以死懼之？若使民常畏死，而為奇者，吾得執而殺之，孰敢？

74. 2. There is always One who presides over the infliction death. He who would inflict death in the room of him who so presides over it may be described as hewing wood instead of a great carpenter. Seldom is it that he who undertakes the hewing, instead of the great carpenter, does not cut his own hands!

常有司殺者殺。夫代司殺者殺，是謂代大匠。夫代大匠斷者，希有不傷其手矣。

CHAPTER 75

貴生章

75. 1. The people suffer from famine because of the multitude of taxes consumed by their superiors. It is through this that they suffer famine.

民之饑，以其上食稅之多，是以饑。

75. 2. The people are difficult to govern because of the (excessive) agency of their superiors (in governing them). It is through this that they are difficult to govern.

民之難治，以其上之有爲，是以難治。

75. 3. The people make light of dying because of the greatness of their labours in seeking for the means of living. It is this which makes them think light of dying. Thus it is that to leave the subject of living altogether out of view is better than to set a high value on it.

民之輕死，以其上求生之厚，是以輕死。夫唯無以生爲者，是賢于貴生。

CHAPTER 76

柔弱章

76. 1. Man at his birth is supple and weak; at his death, firm and strong. (So it is with) all things. Trees and plants, in their early growth, are soft and brittle; at their death, dry and withered.
人之生也柔弱，其死也堅強。萬物草木之生也柔脆，其死也枯槁。

76. 2. Thus it is that firmness and strength are the concomitants of death; softness and weakness, the concomitants of life.
故堅強者死之徒，柔弱者生之徒。

76. 3. Hence he who (relies on) the strength of his forces does not conquer; and a tree which is strong will fill the out-stretched arms, (and thereby invites the feller.)
是以兵強則不勝，木強則兵。

76. 4. Therefore the place of what is firm and strong is below, and that of what is soft and weak is above.
強大處下，柔弱處上。

CHAPTER 77

天道章

77. 1. May not the Way (or Tâo) of Heaven be compared to the (method of) bending a bow? The (part of the bow) which was high is brought low, and what was low is raised up. (So Heaven) diminishes where there is superabundance, and supplements where there is deficiency.

天之道，其猶張弓與！高者抑之，下者舉之；
有餘者損之，不足者補之。

77. 2. It is the Way of Heaven to diminish superabundance, and to supplement deficiency. It is not so with the way of man. He takes away from those who have not enough to add to his own superabundance.

天之道，損有餘而補不足；人之道，則不然，
損不足以奉有餘。

77. 3. Who can take his own superabundance and therewith serve all under heaven? Only he who is in possession of the Tâo!

孰能有余以奉天下？唯有道者。

77. 4. Therefore the (ruling) sage acts without claiming the results as his; he achieves his merit and does not rest (arrogantly) in it:—he does not wish to display his superiority.

是以聖人為而不恃，功成而不處，其不欲見賢。

CHAPTER 78

水德章

78. 1. There is nothing in the world more soft and weak than water, and yet for attacking things that are firm and strong there is nothing that can take precedence of it;—for there is nothing (so effectual) for which it can be changed.

天下莫弱于水，而攻堅強者莫之能勝。以其無以易之。

78. 2. Every one in the world knows that the soft overcomes the hard, and the weak the strong, but no one is able to carry it out in practice.

弱之勝強，柔之勝剛，天下莫不知，莫能行。

78. 3. Therefore a sage has said,
'He who accepts his state's reproach,
Is hailed therefore its altars' lord;
To him who bears men's direful woes
They all the name of King accord.'

是以聖人雲：「受國之垢，是謂社稷主；受國不祥，是謂天下王。」

78. 4. Words that are strictly true seem to be paradoxical.

正言若反。

CHAPTER 79

左契章

79. 1. When a reconciliation is effected (between two parties) after a great animosity, there is sure to be a grudge remaining (in the mind of the one who was wrong). And how can this be beneficial (to the other)?

和大怨，必有余怨，安可以為善？

79. 2. Therefore (to guard against this), the sage keeps the left-hand portion of the record of the engagement, and does not insist on the (speedy) fulfilment of it by the other party. (So), he who has the attributes (of the Tâo) regards (only) the conditions of the engagement, while he who has not those attributes regards only the conditions favourable to himself.

是以聖人執左契，而不責于人。有德司契，無德司澈。

79. 3. In the Way of Heaven, there is no partiality of love; it is always on the side of the good man.

天道無親，常與善人。

CHAPTER 80
不徙章

80. 1. In a little state with a small population, I would so order it, that, though there were individuals with the abilities of ten or a hundred men, there should be no employment of them; I would make the people, while looking on death as a grievous thing, yet not remove elsewhere (to avoid it).
小國寡民，使有什伯之器而不用，使民重死而不遠徙。

80. 2. Though they had boats and carriages, they should have no occasion to ride in them; though they had buff coats and sharp weapons, they should have no occasion to don or use them.
雖有舟輿，無所乘之；雖有甲兵，無所陳之。

80. 3. I would make the people return to the use of knotted cords (instead of the written characters).
使民復結繩而用之。

80. 4. They should think their (coarse) food sweet; their (p
clothes beautiful; their (poor) dwellings places of rest; and
their common (simple) ways sources of enjoyment.

甘其食，美其服，安其居，樂其俗。

80. 5. There should be a neighbouring state within sight, and the
voices of the fowls and dogs should be heard all the way
from it to us, but I would make the people to old age, even to
death, not have any intercourse with it.

鄰國相望，鷄犬之聲相聞，民至老死不相
往來。

CHAPTER 81
不積章

81. 1. Sincere words are not fine; fine words are not sincere. Those who are skilled (in the Tâo) do not dispute (about it); the disputatious are not skilled in it. Those who know (the Tâo) are not extensively learned; the extensively learned do not know it.

信言不美，美言不信。善者不辯，辯者不善。知者不博，博者不知。

81. 2. The sage does not accumulate (for himself). The more that he expends for others, the more does he possess of his own; the more that he gives to others, the more does he have himself.

聖人不積，既以為人已余有，既以與人已愈多。

81. 3. With all the sharpness of the Way of Heaven, it injures not; with all the doing in the way of the sage he does not strive.

天下道，利而不害；聖人之道，為而不爭。